ANTS

ANTS

by Cynthia Overbeck

Photographs by Satoshi Kuribayashi

A Lerner Natural Science Book

Lerner Publications Company ▪ Minneapolis

Sylvia A. Johnson, Series Editor

Translation of original text by Kay Kushion

Additional research by Jane Dallinger

The publisher wishes to thank Jerry W. Heaps.
Department of Entomology, University of Minnesota,
for his assistance in the preparation of this book.

The glossary on page 46 gives definitions and pronunciations
of words shown in **bold type** in the text.

This book is available in two editions:
Library binding by Lerner Publications Company
Soft cover by First Avenue Editions
241 First Avenue North
Minneapolis, Minnesota 55401

LIBRARY OF CONGRESS CATALOGING IN PUBLICATION DATA

Overbeck, Cynthia.
   Ants.

   (A Lerner natural science book)
   Adaptation of: Ari no sekai/by Satoshi Kuribayashi.
   Includes index.
   Summary: Describes the characteristics and be-
havior of ants that build nests for storing food and
raising their young, ants that spend most of their time
traveling, and ants that invade the nests of other ants.
   1. Ants—Juvenile literature. [1. Ants] I. Kuribayashi,
Satoshi, 1939- ill. II. Kuribayashi, Satoshi, 1939-
Ari no sekai. English. III. Title. IV. Series.
QL568.F7093   595.79′6   81-17216
ISBN 0-8225-1468-0 (lib. bdg.)   AACR2

This edition first published 1982 by Lerner Publications Company.
Text copyright © 1982 by Lerner Publications Company.
Photographs copyright © 1971 by Satoshi Kuribayashi.
Adapted from ANTS AND THEIR WORLD copyright © 1971 by Satoshi Kuribayashi.
English language rights arranged by Kurita-Bando Literary Agency
for Akane Shobo Publishers, Tokyo, Japan.

International Standard Book Number: 0-8225-1468-0 (lib. bdg.)
International Standard Book Number: 0-8225-9525-7 (pbk.)
Library of Congress Catalog Card Number: 81-17216

5 6 7 8 9 10 90 89 88 87

No matter where you walk — in a meadow, a forest, a garden, or on a city street — there is one creature you are almost sure to find. This insect is so common that most people barely notice it as it runs busily about. Yet in many ways it is one of the world's most fascinating animals.

This busy insect is, of course, the ant. Beneath the ground, right under our feet, communities of these little insects lead bustling and often dramatic lives. Ants always seem to be in motion. They build complicated nests with dozens of rooms and tunnels. They carry loads many times their own weight.

They watch over their young with great care, feeding them constantly. Sometimes they fight fierce battles among themselves or with enemy ant communities.

Ants carry on these activities almost everywhere in the world, except in the very cold climates of the Arctic, the Antarctic, and some high mountain regions. Within the ant family (Formicidae), there are about 10,000 different species, or kinds, of ants. Each species has its own special habits and physical characteristics. Some species of ants can be as big as 2½ inches (75 centimeters) long. Others are so tiny they can barely be seen. Some may have long, curved jaws; others have broad, square heads. Even ants of the same species can have different sizes and shapes. But no matter what their species, all ants have the same basic body structure.

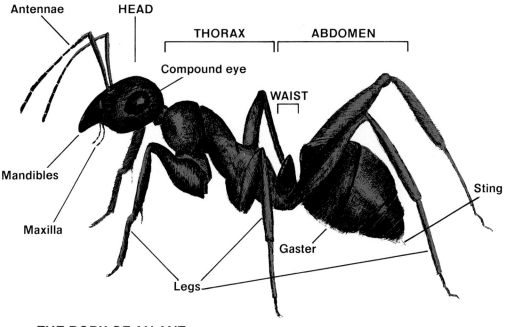

Antennae HEAD THORAX ABDOMEN Compound eye WAIST Mandibles Maxilla Sting Gaster Legs

THE BODY OF AN ANT

Like all insects, ants have three main body parts: the **head, thorax,** and **abdomen.** On an ant's head are all its important sense organs. Most ants have two **compound eyes.** Each is made up of from 6 to 1,000 tiny individual eyes. These eyes help the ant to see its nearby surroundings, as well as any moving objects. Some ants also have 3 extra simple eyes, called **ocelli** (oh-SELL-ee), on top of their heads. These eyes are especially sensitive to light and dark.

This combination of eyes gives many ants good vision. But other ants are totally blind. They find their way around by using their sharp senses of touch and smell.

An ant uses its front leg to clean its antenna.

Ants touch and smell things with their two long, thin **antennae** (an-TEN-ee). These are among the ant's most important sense organs. With its antennae, an ant can detect flavors and sounds, as well as odors. Ants also use their antennae in special ways to communicate with each other. The antennae have 9 to 13 tiny joints that allow them to bend and move easily. Ants are always waving their antennae in the air to pick up odors. They also tap them on objects or on the ground in order to identify something or to feel their way along.

To keep these important organs clean and operating well, some ants have tiny brushes on their front legs. They often stop and brush their antennae carefully until they are cleared of all dirt and water.

On either side of an ant's mouth are special jaws called **mandibles** (MAN-dih-b'ls). These jaws work almost like tongs or pincers. They usually have a jagged, sawtoothed surface. Ants use their mandibles to pick up pieces of food, other ants, and whatever else they need to carry. They also use them as tools to dig nests in the earth or in wood and as weapons for fighting. For chewing their food, ants have another set of smaller jaws, called **maxillae** (mak-SIL-ee), just behind the mandibles.

This closeup photograph of a carpenter ant shows the strong mandibles, as well as the two large compound eyes and the three tiny ocelli located on top of the head.

This ant is licking sweet liquid produced by insects called aphids. The liquid will be stored in the ant's crop.

The ant's three pairs of legs are connected to the thorax, the middle part of its body. Two tiny claws on the end of each leg help the ant to crawl upside down on the ceiling of a room or straight up a blade of tall grass. Sometimes the claws are also used to dig tunnels in the ground. In some special kinds of ants, two pairs of wings are also attached to the thorax.

The thorax is joined to the abdomen by a slender waist. This is a special body feature that allows the ant to bend easily when crawling through the narrow, twisted tunnels of its nest.

In the abdomen's back section, or **gaster,** are two stomachs. The largest, called the **crop,** is a "community" stomach. The ant actually shares the food in this stomach with other ants in its community. As an ant collects food and eats it, the food is dissolved into a liquid and stored in the crop. When a fellow ant is hungry, it strokes the food-gathering ant's head in a certain way with its antennae. The two ants then put their mouths together, and the liquid food passes from the food-gatherer to the hungry ant.

In addition to the crop, each ant has another, smaller, stomach in its gaster. This is the ant's "personal" stomach. When a food-gathering ant needs nourishment for itself, some of the food in its crop is passed into this stomach and digested.

**Two ants
sharing food**

Left: Two carpenter ants point the ends of their gasters at each other during a fight. *Right:* Poison droplets can be seen on the upright ends of these ants' gasters.

The ant's gaster also contains poison glands. Some ants eject poison through stingers in the ends of their gasters. Other ants have no stingers but can squirt a poisonous acid at their enemies through a tiny opening in the rear of the gaster. Only a few kinds of ants have a poison strong enough to cause pain in humans. But ant poison can paralyze enemy ants and even insects like caterpillars that are much larger than the ants.

An individual ant is an insect with great strength and energy. But ants cannot live as individuals. Their whole existence depends on the way they live as a group. This is why ants are called "social" insects. In order for one ant to survive, it must work together with other ants. Ants must help each other to find food, to take care of their young, and to defend the group from enemies. It takes many ants together, each doing its own special job, to keep the community alive.

A group of ants living together in this way is called a **colony.** Ant colonies may contain only a few dozen members, or more than a million. The colony is made up of three main kinds of adult ants—one or more **queens,** a few males, and many, many female **workers.** Sometimes there are special female workers called **soldiers,** too.

A queen is the largest ant in the colony. She is usually several times as large as the workers. Her duty in the colony is to mate and to lay eggs. Her eggs contain all the future workers, males, soldiers, and new queens needed to keep the colony going. The few males in the colony have only one duty—mating with a queen and fertilizing her eggs.

All the rest of the work—building the nest, caring for the young, gathering food, and defending the nest—is done by the tireless little workers. Sometimes they get help from the soldiers, which are extra-large workers with big heads and powerful jaws. These ants guard and defend the nest and sometimes help to bring in food.

The pictures here and on the next few pages show carpenter ants mating and raising their young. *Left:* This carpenter ant queen is so heavy that she cannot get off the ground. *Right:* In order to begin her mating flight, the queen climbs up on a leaf and jumps off into the air.

How do ant colonies get started? A new colony is always formed by a queen that has hatched in an existing colony. At certain times of the year, the queen of an established colony lays eggs that develop into new young queens and males. After these **reproductive** ants grow to maturity, they are ready to mate. This usually happens during the warm summer months.

As if by a signal, there is a sudden increase of activity in the nest. The workers begin to crawl around excitedly. They push the queens and the males outside. The reproductive ants are not hard to spot, for they are the only ones with wings. The wings are used just once, for the mating flight.

Once all the winged males and queens are outside, it is time for the flight to begin.

14

Small, wingless carpenter workers crawl excitedly around the winged males and a huge queen (seen in the upper left part of the picture).

A male carpenter ant dies after mating with a queen.

During the mating flight, each queen mates with a single male. When the males have mated, their one duty in life has been fulfilled. They are no longer needed, and they fall to the ground, where they die or are eaten by animals.

But a queen's duties are just beginning. After mating, she is capable of laying thousands of eggs during a lifetime that may last from 5 years to as much as 15 years. Now she must find a place to lay her eggs where they will be safe from animals that may want to eat them.

First, the queen must get rid of her wings. She has no more use for them, because she will spend the rest of her life inside her nest. So she rubs the wings against a stone and tugs at them with her jaws. Finally, when they have come off, she looks for a nesting place.

A queen carpenter ant sheds her wings after mating.

Sometimes a queen will return to the nest from which she came. If it is a large nest, it may have room for more than one queen. In other cases, a new queen may be welcomed into the nest of an existing colony that has no queen of its own. And sometimes, the queen of a warlike species may invade an established colony, kill its queen, and take over.

But most often, the queen must start a new colony of her own. All alone, she uses her jaws and claws to dig a small nest for herself. Depending on her species, she may dig into the earth, a rotten log, or the twig of a living tree.

The queen burrows into her nest and seals the entrance behind her. Safe inside, she lays her first few eggs. While she waits for these eggs to hatch, the queen will not be able to leave the nest to eat. She must spend several weeks or even months without food. During this time, she lives on her own body fat and on nutrients that are released into her body from the large wing muscles she no longer needs. Often she must eat some of her smallest eggs in order to stay alive. Eating these eggs also helps to make sure that the eggs still in her body will have nourishment.

Eggs are the first stage in the four-part life cycle of an ant, which is known as **metamorphosis** (met-uh-MOR-fuh-sis). During metamorphosis, an ant goes through four complete changes in form. These four stages are **egg, larva, pupa** (PEW-puh), and **adult.** Ants of most species take about three months to go through the whole cycle from egg to adult.

A queen carpenter ant tends her first eggs.

Left: The first white worker ants appear in a carpenter ant nest. *Right:* The pupae of the carpenter ants are cared for by the queen and her workers. The worker on the left is tending a pile of eggs.

The queen ant's eggs are white and very tiny—smaller than pinheads. As her first eggs grow, she tends them carefully and keeps them clean by licking them constantly. In about 20 days, the young hatch from their eggs and enter the second stage of metamorphosis—the larva stage. Ant larvae (LAR-vee) are soft, worm-like white grubs. They are blind and have no legs. The queen continues to wash them and must now feed them with nutrients from her own body.

After about a month, the larvae shed their skins. Some species spin a **cocoon** (kuh-KOON), or protective covering, around themselves, while others lie naked and exposed. Now they are in the pupa stage. In this stage, the young do not eat. Those without cocoons look like white infant ants. They lie helplessly on their backs with their legs curled up.

After another 20 days or so, the development of the young ants is complete. If the pupae are in cocoons, the queen helps to tear the covering away. The young ants that come out are called **callows.** These small, pale-colored ants will darken in color as they mature. They are the first workers of the new colony.

Immediately the new workers go into action. They seem to know that their job is to dig out of the nest as soon as possible in order to find food for their queen. They bring back the nourishing bodies of insects or fat seeds for her to feast on.

At last the queen's lonely wait is over. From now on, the workers will take care of her. They will bring her food, care for her constant supply of new eggs, and extend the nest. Most workers lead short lives compared to the queen—from only a few weeks to five or six years at the most. But more workers will replace the first ones, and the colony will grow.

A worker helps the carpenter queen to tend her eggs, larvae, and pupae. From now on the queen's only job will be to lay precious eggs for the colony.

These hills of dirt mark the entrances to ant nests.

As more and more workers hatch, they all begin to scurry around, doing the many jobs that are necessary in the colony. One of the most important jobs is that of enlarging the nest. Ants build their nests in all kinds of places. Some species, called carpenter ants, chew tunnels in the damp, rotten wood of logs or telephone poles. Other species nest in the branches or twigs of living trees. The most familiar kinds of ants dig their nests in the earth.

An earth nest begins with the single small room that the queen made before she laid her eggs. First, the workers dig a series of underground tunnels leading out of the original room. Using their jaws and their front claws, they dig out the dirt piece by piece and carry it up to the surface. Some species of ants then haul the dirt away and scatter it around. Others let it pile up around the entrance to the nest.

Almost everyone has seen little hills of dirt in sidewalk cracks or in open fields. These surround the entrances to the ants' underground nests. Usually they are very small hills of loose dirt. But some ants, such as the harvesters, build hills that average 2 feet (60 centimeters) tall and are hard-packed. In Africa, the hills formed by the nests of some species grow to enormous size over the years. One hill was reported to be 25 feet (7.5 meters) tall!

In the ground beneath the anthills, and sometimes within the hills themselves, many new rooms and tunnel systems are dug by the industrious workers. In a typical nest there are many rooms, each with a special use. One room is reserved for the queen. There she stays, laying a constant supply of eggs and being watched over, fed, and cleaned by the workers.

Other rooms serve as "nurseries" for the eggs, larvae, and pupae. Workers carry the newly laid eggs in piles to these rooms. There nurse workers take care of the young. They clean and feed the larvae and help the pupae when they are ready to come out of their cocoons. There are many nursery rooms throughout the nest, and the nurses are always moving the young around to find the warmest, driest spots on any given day. Sometimes, in warm weather, they even carry the young outside the nest to air them in the sun.

Still other rooms in the nest are used as resting places for the workers or as storerooms for food. During the winter,

AN UNDERGROUND ANT NEST

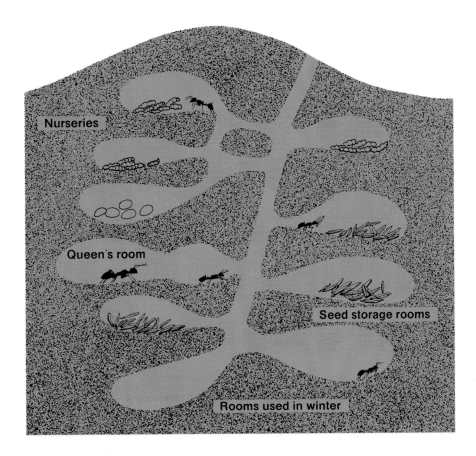

Nurseries

Queen's room

Seed storage rooms

Rooms used in winter

ants that live in cold climates stay in the rooms that are farthest underground and therefore the least likely to freeze. Protected from the extreme cold, these ants spend the winter months in the inactive state of **hibernation.**

Opposite: **A worker carries a load of dirt out of its nest.**

Right: **This ant is drinking the sweet nectar of a thistle flower.**

In addition to building the nest and caring for the queen and the young, worker ants have the all-important job of gathering food for the colony. Ants eat many foods. They get sugars from plant juices and sweet liquids. They get protein from the bodies of insects and animals.

Many kinds of ants are predators, or hunters. They attack and eat bees, beetles, caterpillars, and other insects. Other ants, such as the harvester ants, lead a quieter life as seed-gatherers. Still other species protect small insects like aphids in exchange for the opportunity to eat a sweet liquid produced by the aphids' bodies.

Two ants attack an insect many times bigger than themselves.

Left: These lucky ants have found a piece of candy. *Right:* Black ants attack a may beetle.

In some species such as the harvesters, individual workers scurry about on their own. They pick up seeds where they find them and return them to the nest. In other species, a few "scout" workers leave the nest first to search for food. When they find something too large for them to handle alone, such as a large insect or a big piece of candy, they rush back to the nest.

A column of ants marches back and forth along a fixed path.

The scouts "tell" other workers about their find by tapping them excitedly with their antennae. Some of the workers get the "message" and hurry out to find the food. Soon, a regular route is established between the food and the nest, and all the ants follow it. It is a common sight to see ants scurrying back and forth in a line, almost as though they are on a tiny two-lane highway.

Red soldier and worker ants attack a black ant. The large,
square-headed ant with the big jaws is the soldier.

**This ant is stinging a
weevil to paralyze it.**

Team effort is especially needed when the ants take on a large insect. In some species, the little worker ants get help from the soldier ants. These ants are bigger than the ordinary workers, and their larger, stronger jaws are better designed for biting. To overcome a large caterpillar or other insect, many ants get together and attack from all sides. They bite and then sting or spray the victim with poison to paralyze it. When the victim finally dies, it is torn to small pieces and carried back to the nest. The hardy workers that do this job can sometimes carry loads of food more than 50 times their own weight. That would be roughly the same as a person lifting a small elephant!

Carpenter worker ants with a beetle they have killed.

A ladybug attacks and eats aphids.

Not all ants kill the insects they find. Some have an unusual habit of drinking the sweet liquid produced by the bodies of certain insects. One such insect is the tiny **aphid** (A-fid). Aphids attach themselves to plant leaves, roots, and flowers, where they suck the sap. The aphids' bodies then produce a sweet "honeydew" from the sap. When an ant taps an aphid with its antenna, a drop of this honeydew is released. The hungry ant then licks it up. Sometimes groups of ants watch over whole "herds" of aphids and "milk" them almost like dairy cows.

In return for the honeydew, the ants clean the aphids and protect them from insect predators like the ladybug. They may even take aphid eggs into their nests over the winter and care for them. In the spring, they move the new adult aphids onto the juiciest plant leaves and roots. There the ant workers line up and lick honeydew from the row of aphids. The workers store this honeydew in their crops and take it back to share with other ants in the nest.

Ants "milk" a row of aphids on a leaf.

Harvester ants carry seeds back to their nests.

Many ants depend on seeds for food. The harvester ants work busily all summer long collecting seeds for winter storage. These are probably the ants that inspired the Aesop fable about the lazy grasshopper and the hard-working ant. The harvester ants certainly are industrious. They build very complicated nests with many rooms and tunnels for storing their grain and their young. Their anthills are an average of 2 feet (60 centimeters) high and 2 to 5 feet (60 to 150 centimeters) in diameter. The total number of rooms underground and in the hills themselves may be as many as 400.

The workers go out singly to search for seeds. Each struggles back to the nest carrying its heavy load. At the nest entrance, large-jawed soldiers help to tear the hulls from the seeds. Then the seeds are carried down to storage rooms within the nest. These rooms, which are usually about an inch (2.5 centimeters) high and 3 to 6 inches (7.5 to 15 centimeters) long, become filled with seeds from every imaginable kind of flowering plant.

Most ant colonies thrive by dividing all necessary jobs among the hardworking soldiers and workers. But some types of ants don't work at all. Instead, they get other ants to do their work for them. These ants are known as "slave-makers." Japanese samurai (SAM-uh-ri), or warrior, ants are one type that cannot carry on a successful colony by themselves. Samurai ants are large and strong, with powerful mandibles. But their mandibles are smooth and pointed, suitable only for fighting. They do not have the useful jagged edges needed for important digging and carrying. The samurai cannot even feed themselves. So they get slaves to feed them, take care of their young, and keep their nests in good order.

During the warm summer months, a gang of samurai ants may make a surprise raid on a colony of black ants. They force their way into the nest. Thrown into panic and confusion, the weaker black ants can do little. The samurai grab

42

the black ants' larvae and pupae in their jaws and hurry off to their own nests. There, the samurai keep the kidnapped young until they mature. When the young black ants become workers, they will serve as slaves for the samurai, feeding them from their crops and doing all the other tasks around the nest.

Slave-makers, as well as other ants, do a great deal of fighting with ants of enemy colonies, and sometimes even with members of their own colonies. Ants are one of the few creatures besides humans that kill and enslave their own kind. Usually two colonies will battle each other over food. They also fight over territory, especially when the nest of one colony is too close to the nest of another. Individual ants from the same colony may also fight over a tasty bit of food.

The opponents bite and sting each other and squirt poison from their gasters. Usually such fights are fierce, and they last until one or the other ant is dead.

Left: A black ant fights with a much smaller red ant. *Right:* A conflict between two black ants.

People usually think of ants as pests that spoil picnics and invade kitchens. And it is true that ants can sometimes be destructive. Those that build many large anthills can make a farmer's field useless for growing crops or grazing animals. Some ants protect aphids, which in turn damage trees and plants. Other ants inflict painful stings and bites on humans and animals.

But most ants are helpful to people. They eat many insect pests that are harmful to crops and orchards. In turn, ants themselves serve as food for other insects and for spiders, frogs, and birds. And their underground tunnels help to make the soil healthy by letting air circulate through it.

Whether they help or harm humans, ants have a place in the world, like all other living creatures. By observing and studying these insects, we can learn something about a fascinating part of the natural world.

GLOSSARY

abdomen — the rear section of an ant's body

antenna (plural *antennae*) — the feeler on an ant's head, used to detect odors, flavors, and sounds. An ant's sense of touch is also in its antennae.

aphid — a tiny insect that eats the sap of plant roots, leaves, and flowers

callow — a newly emerged ant, not entirely hardened or fully colored

cocoon — a white covering spun by some ant pupae for protection

colony — an organized group of ants living together and sharing work duties

compound eyes — large eyes made up of 6 to 1000 tiny lenses

crop — the ant's "community" stomach. Ants share the food in this stomach with other ants in the colony.

egg — the first stage in metamorphosis. Ant eggs are sticky, white, and smaller than a pinhead.

gaster — the rear section of an ant's abdomen

hibernate — to spend the winter in an inactive state during which all the body functions slow down

46

larva (plural *larvae*)—the second stage in metamorphosis. Ant larvae are white, legless grubs.

mandibles—the two jaws on either side of the ant's mouth, used for digging, carrying, and fighting

maxillae—two smaller jaws used for chewing food

metamorphosis—the life cycle of an ant, in which the insect goes through four complete changes in form: egg, larva, pupa, and adult.

ocelli—small, simple eyes found on the heads of some ant species

pupa (plural *pupae*)—the third stage in metamorphosis. Some ant pupae spin a cocoon around themselves in this stage.

queen—the fertile female ant in a colony, capable of laying all the colony's eggs.

reproductive ants—ants able to mate and produce young. Only queens and males are capable of reproduction.

soldier—a large, strong-jawed type of worker ant, especially suited for fighting

thorax—the middle section of an ant's body, between the head and abdomen

worker—a small female ant that does all the work of the colony

INDEX

abdomen, 10-12
antennae, 8
anthills, 24, 39, 45
aphids, 27, 36, 45

black ants, 42-43
body of ant, 7; abdomen, 10-12;
    head, 6, 8-9; thorax, 10

callows, 21
carpenter ants, 23; pictures of,
    14-17, 19, 22
cocoons, 20, 21
colony, ant, 13, 18, 42;
    establishment of, 14, 18
compound eyes, 6
crop, 10-11

damage caused by ants, 45

eggs, 13, 18, 20, 24
eyes, 6

fighting among ants, 44
food gathering, 27, 30-31, 33,
    36, 39
food sharing, 11

gaster, 10, 11, 12

harvester ants, 24, 27, 30, 39
hibernation, 25

kinds of ants, 6

larva, 18, 20, 24
life cycle of ant, 18, 20-21
life span of ant, 12, 22

male ants, 13, 14, 17
mandibles, 9, 42

mating, 14, 17
maxillae, 9
metamorphosis, 18, 20-21

nests, 17, 18, 39; building of,
    23-24; rooms of, 22-25, 39
nurseries in ant nests, 24

ocelli, 6

places where ants live, 6
poison, ant, 12, 33, 34
predators, ants as, 27, 33
pupa, 18, 20-21, 24

queen, 13, 18, 24; mating of, 14,
    17; role of, in caring for young,
    18, 20, 21, 22; role of, in
    establishing colony, 14

reproductive ants, 14

samurai ants, 42-43
seed gathering, 27, 30, 39
sense organs, 8
simple eyes, 6
sizes of ants, 6
slave-making ants, 42-43, 44
social insects, ants as, 13
soldiers, 13, 33, 39
stinger, 12
stomach, 10-11

thorax, 6, 10

workers, 13, 14; development of,
    20-21; as nurses, 24; role of, in
    food-gathering, 27, 30-31, 33,
    36, 39; role of, in nest building,
    23